Old WEST LINTON

with Carlops, Lamancha, Romanno Bridge, Mountain Cross, Blyth Bridge
by
T.C. Atkinson

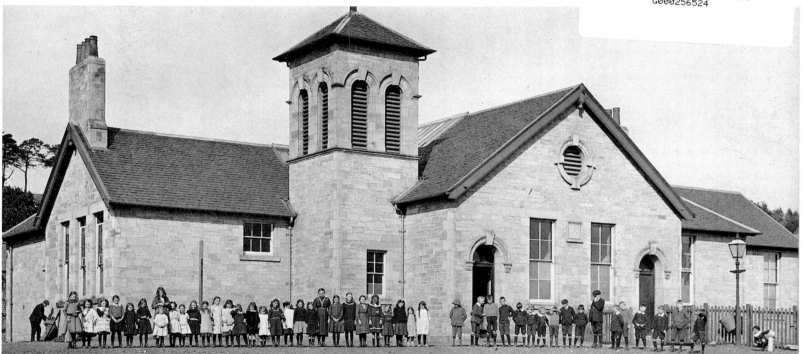

The succession of schools in West Linton is rather confusing, mainly due to the three churches in the village each at one time running their own schools. This was all changed under the Scottish Education Act of 1872 which established a central authority to oversee the universal provision of education. Locally, this eventually resulted in the transferring of the parish school of 1864 in Main Street to the larger premises of the Somerville School, now St Andrew's Large Church Hall, in 1891. From there the school moved to its present site on School Brae and the photograph shows the new building shortly after its opening in 1907. The school has had several extensions since, but apart from the tower which was removed decades ago, what is seen here remains although incorporated in the present buildings.

Text © T.C. Atkinson, 2002.
First published in the United Kingdom, 2002,
by Stenlake Publishing,
Telephone / Fax: 01290 551122

ISBN 1 84033 208 5

FURTHER READING

The books listed below were used by the author during his research. None of them are available from Stenlake Publishing. Those interested in finding out more are advised to contact their local bookshop or reference library.
The Third Statistical Account of Scotland, The County of Peebles, 1964.
Robert Brown, *The Works of Alexander Pennecuik*, 1815.
J.W. Buchan & Rev. H. Paton, *The History of Peeblesshire*, 1927.
Rev. Alexander Forrester, *The New Statistical Account of Peeblesshire*, 1834.
Kirkurd WRI, *History of Kirkurd*, 1966.
Newlands WRI, *History of Newlands*, 1966.

ACKNOWLEDGEMENTS

The author would like to thank West Linton Historical Association for the use of material from the Village Archive, including a number of photographs used in this book; also Rae Montgomery for the information relating to the railway photographs and for suggested amendments to the text; and to all those who have given him support and encouragement, especially his wife Jeanette without whose help this book may not have been completed on time.

The publishers wish to thank Robert Grieves for supplying the picture on the inside front cover.

Opposite the Raemartin Hotel in West Linton is a cottage which has on its gable wall this remarkable carved stone panel dating from 1666, when it was carved by James Gifford, a local worthy. He built and lived in a two storey house next to the site occupied by this cottage and, besides his talent as a sculptor, was a self-proclaimed 'architector'. The central panel shows on the left a self-portrait inscribed 'JAMES GIFFERD' and on the right a portrait of his wife 'EWPHAM VEATCH'. In the same year Gifford took up arms on the side of the Covenanters at the Battle of Rullion Green and is said to have sheltered afterwards under the Harbour Craig, a large rock near Carlops where his initials can be seen.

INTRODUCTION

Evidence of prehistoric man is still being found in the hills surrounding West Linton in the form of artifacts, monuments and places of settlement, suggesting that humans have been shaping this landscape since the earliest times. There are signs of Stone Age settlement in the form of flint chippings and flint knives, and the impressive structures of Nether Cairn and Upper Cairn to the west of Mendick Hill date from the Bronze Age. A few years ago an extensive cemetery was unearthed at West Water Reservoir where the graves revealed pottery and jewellery made by early farmers. Iron Age hut sites can be seen on the lower slopes of the Pentlands and forts dominate many of the hilltops beside the Lyne Water, especially below Romanno Bridge. Later, the Romans came via Clydesdale and crossed the foothills of the Pentlands, passing Dolphinton, West Linton and Carlops. They also came up the Lyne Valley from their fort at Lyne and passed Kirkurd on their way to Castledykes.

The early name of West Linton – 'West' being an eighteenth century addition – was *Lyntunrudderic*, perhaps after Rydderck Hael (Roderick the Liberal), the Christian King of Strathclyde who died in AD 603. The village did not appear in written records until the twelfth century when Richard Comyn created a charter granting the monks of St Mary of Kelso the village's church along with 'a half ploughgate of land'. The Comyns, a Norman family, were succeeded as landowners by the Morton Douglases in the fourteenth century. This family eventually came to own almost all of the parish, but suffered a temporary eclipse after the execution in 1581 of the famous Regent Morton who built Drochil Castle. They also built the Manor House – probably the oldest building in the village – at the head of Main Street in 1578, and the tradition for stone carving which the village acquired probably started with the masons from Drochil.

In 1631 William, sixth Earl of Morton, sold all his Peeblesshire lands to Sir John Stewart who became first Earl of Traquair. In the same year Sir John received a Crown charter making the lands a free barony of regality. It was not long, however, before this family fell into debt and in 1663 John, second Earl of Traquair, sold the lands to Andrew Rutherford, first Lord Rutherford and Earl of Teviot.

In 1664 power was given to hold a weekly market in the village every Wednesday and two annual fairs in July and September. Initially, these took place on the site of the Lower Green, but eventually, as trade grew, they moved to near the Bridgehouse Inn, now Medwyn House.

Probably from as early as the fifteenth century cattle were being driven to England and certainly by the early eighteenth century West Linton would have witnessed the passage of cattle on their way south. The great trysts at Crieff (and later Falkirk) were the main centre of cattle sales for nearly two centuries and the drove route to the English markets headed south to the Cauldstane Slap in the Pentland Hills and then on through West Linton to Romanno Bridge and Peebles. The route of this drove road is clearly seen in places below the Cauldstane Slap, at Baddinsgill and in the hills above Romanno Bridge.

The Roman road between Dolphinton and Carlops continued to be used throughout medieval times and along it history passed by West Linton. Edward I, on his way to Ayr in 1298 after doing battle with Wallace at Falkirk, was a most unwelcome visitor, and Sir John Comyn and Sir Simon Fraser of Neidpath went by in 1302 on their way to do battle at Roslin. In 1490 James IV was cheered as he came through and Mary, Queen of Scots, hurried by in 1567. In 1666 Covenanting survivors from the battle at Rullion Green were given shelter in the isolated cottages in the hills above the village. While in exile at Holyrood in 1830, Charles X of France came to shoot on the moor at Slipperfield while staying at Bridgehouse. Fifty years earlier, while on his way to Edinburgh, Robert Burns is said to have visited the Bridgehouse Inn to see his friend Robert Graham. Twice unable to find him at home he scratched these words on a pane in the inn: 'Honest Graham, aye the same, never to be found at hame.'

The tradition of weaving was strong in West Linton and in 1791 there were two dozen looms, rising to forty in 1840 when cotton was woven for sale in Glasgow. West Linton was at that time regarded as a weaving village and the weavers' cottages still stand in Main Street. Coal was mined since the beginning of the eighteenth century on the moor to the east of the village and there was also a quarry for limestone at Whitfield where, in 1834, considerable quantities of good quality lime were produced. This was used in the land improvement that was taking place around the village at that time. Enclosing land, draining marshy areas, planting trees for shelter, liming the ground, building farm houses, introducing turnips for winter feed and improving roads and bridges were all measures adopted locally by the new owners as part of this improvement.

Until 1870 white freestone quarrying was carried out extensively at Deepsykehead (this stone was used to build the Glen, the mansion south of Traquair) and red sandstone was quarried at Broomlee and provided stone for several houses in the village.

In 1864 the railway came to West Linton. Although this did not attract any new industry, it did put the village on the map for visitors and some of them fell for its charm and settled here. Even though the railway is now long gone, the charm remains and the village has become a thriving community.

Miss Helen Fergusson, youngest daughter of Sir William Fergusson (Queen Victoria's surgeon), was the Secretary of the Broomlee Band of Mercy. The branch first met in 1891, on the anniversary of Queen Victoria's Coronation, and by 1895, when this photograph was taken, there was no shortage of members. To celebrate Queen Victoria's Diamond Jubilee in 1897 the Band of Mercy decided to raise money for the provision of a drinking place for 'thirsty and wearied horses passing through the village' and one of their efforts was to hold a bazaar at Broomlee House. Their fund-raising was obviously successful as the drinking place, a handsome cast iron horse trough, was acquired and can still be seen near the Bogsbank Road bridge which, when it was built to replace the ford, deprived the horses of a drink in the river. The photograph shows the Band of Mercy outside Broomlee House, the home of the Misses Fergusson, who are standing beside their front door.

BROOMLEE RESIDENTIAL SCHOOL CAMP, WEST LINTON.

A lot of people's memories of West Linton date from when they came as school children to the summer camp at Broomlee. Broomlee was one of five residential schools set up before the Second World War where children from other counties, mainly Ayrshire, Midlothian, Fife and Lanarkshire, came with their teachers to study, play and live together. In 1940 evacuees from Edinburgh were its first occupants and since then thousands of young people, including some from abroad, have enjoyed its amenities. This postcard, sent in August 1952, reads 'Having a lovely time although it rained all day yesterday. This morning we are going to church. In the afternoon we are going on a hike and in the evening we are having 'Twenty Questions'. I am quite well now.'

Broomlee Station in the 1920s. On the left is the signalman's house and in the garden his daughter, Jean Fleming, who later became a school teacher and local historian who wrote many articles on country life in Peeblesshire. The railway brought much prosperity to West Linton and was greatly responsible for its development. By 1912 eighty houses in the village provided accommodation for visitors and with a journey time to Edinburgh Waverley of forty-seven minutes it is not surprising that Edinburgh people found West Linton the perfect holiday place. Some families bought houses locally or built new villas so that they could stay throughout the summer while the breadwinner travelled daily to the city. This all came to an end in 1933 when the line closed to passenger traffic. A spectacular accident happened in 1948 when several empty goods wagons broke loose at Macbiehill and set off downhill for the two miles to the end of the line. By then this had become a coalyard and the wagons ploughed on through the gates, across the road, and ended up in a heap at the old station. The incident was witnessed by a nanny and her charges and it was fortunate that nobody was hurt.

The Leadburn, Linton and Dolphinton Railway opened on 4 July 1864 with no ceremony, although the villagers would certainly have been there to witness the event. Its Engineer was the Englishman Thomas Bouch who had a reputation for designing railways cheaply to meet local needs. He had been Engineer for the Peebles Railway which opened in 1855 and was later the designer of the ill-fated Tay Bridge. The railway was not an immediate financial success as the hoped for mineral traffic from the coal mines and limestone quarries never materialised. The line was taken over by the North British Railway in July 1866. This picture, taken at the turn of the century, shows the staff of Broomlee, the name adopted in order to avoid confusion with East Linton, outside the stationmaster's house. *Back row* (left to right): Tom Cowe, clerk; Bob Miller, porter; Joe Joss, stationmaster; John Fleming, signalman. *Front row*: Fred Dickson, Eck Niddrie and Philip Somerville, surfacemen.

In the foreground of this view of Church Corner is the cast iron horse trough given by the Broomlee Band of Mercy. It was moved here before the First World War from its position in front of the Raemartin Hotel. The ornate lamp-post beside it was also paid for by public subscription. The toll-house on the left, set at an angle to accommodate the road junction, was built around 1756, at the time of much needed improvements to the Edinburgh–Moffat road. St Andrew's Church was built in 1782 and enlarged in 1871 when the steeple was added and the roof was raised to accommodate a gallery. In front of the church stands the memorial to the thirty-two men of the parish who gave their lives in the First World War. The elaborate electricity poles are a reminder that electricity came to the village in 1931, shortly before this photograph was taken.

A parade celebrating the coronation of George V in 1911, about to pass Fairley Villa in Main Street. This is the present manse. One of the first cars in the village was that of Mr Robertson, who lived in Fairley Villa, and on one occasion, accompanied by Robert Sanderson – otherwise known as the 'Laureate of Lynedale', West Linton's famous poet – he drove to Wanlockhead and back in one day. For such a historic event the whole school was allowed to turn out to watch the car's progress up Main Street!

The children in this view of Main Street are standing outside the police station, which served the village from this site until a new station was built on Bogsbank Road in the 1960s. Opposite, on the other side of the road, are the premises of a tobacconist which was later occupied by Robert Slimmand, fruiterer and florist. Just beyond can be seen the corner of 'The Ark', one of the few original cottages which would at one time have made up most of Main Street. The shops under the 'Teas' signs were a stationer and a tearoom run by Misses Stoddart and Taylor who offered 'dainty service' and 'confections by leading makers'. Further up the street the building with the dormer windows was originally the Parish School until its closure in 1891. It was then converted into a shop with a dwelling house above.

A village tap and gas lamp holder can be seen here in front of the premises of Archibald Bain, Boot and Shoemaker of Main Street. There had been a long tradition of making boots in West Linton, indeed the village produced a style of shepherd's boot, with a distinct upturned toe, which was very popular. This firm was still in business in 1912 in premises at the end of Deanfoot Road. The building pictured is now known as Townfoot House, a reminder of the limits of the village in earlier times.

This view of Main Street in the last quarter of the nineteenth century shows, on the right, the Parish School (before its conversion), which opened in 1864 with its distinctive belfry standing high above the village. Next to it is what was probably one of the few remaining thatched weavers' cottages in the village. On the left is Lyne Villa, now Bank House, shortly after its construction on the site of William Melrose's house, a building which had stood since the seventeenth century. The statue of 'Lady' Gifford can be seen standing on the Cross Well against the right-hand gable beyond the iron railings, the position where she was moved to in 1861.

This view of Main Street from 1913 shows on the right the shop of Alexander Fraser who established his business as 'Pharmacist, Chemist and Dentist' ten years earlier. There was another chemist's shop in the village at this time – The Pharmacy – which was further down Main Street, opposite the 'Old Police Station'. The shop behind the clock is that of James Gordon, tailor and clothier, who established his business in 1889 and specialised in ladies costumes. He was also a newsagent and agent for 'Messrs. J. Pullar & Son, Cleaners & Dyers, Perth.' At the far end, in the centre of the picture, are the premises of David Patterson, Wine, Spirit and General Merchant, established in 1891 and who advertised 'First quality of family groceries and provisions always at hand'. At two o'clock on a grey afternoon the street looks very quiet in comparison with today. The many shops reflect the expansion in the higher parts of the village which followed the upgrading of the water supply in 1898.

Standing in Main Street, on the site of the old Cross Well at the centre of the village, is the Clock. The figure at the front on the pedestal is that of 'Lady' Gifford, wife of James Gifford, who in 1666 carved this statue to serve as a market cross by placing her upon the well with small statues of their four children at the corners. The arrival of a fifth child presented a problem, which the sculptor solved by placing a statue of the child on its mother's head, an arrangement which caused much amusement to eighteenth century visitors to the village. After being vandalised, the statue was removed and then re-erected in 1861. In 1894 the well was heightened with the incorporation of the parish school clock and 'Lady' Gifford was given the more dignified position shown in the picture. After suffering the ravages of time the statue was replaced with a replica in November 2001, the original being moved into the Graham Institute.

A group of locals posing at one of the village taps in front of Leven Cottage at the head of Lower Green. The taps were introduced after Rumbling Tam, a spring near the Upper Green, was tamed and his efficacious waters – on sale at ½d. a glass on market days – were pumped, for the benefit of the whole community, to a tank set in the hillside above the stables of the Gordon Arms. This took place in 1875 and, coupled with earlier drainage improvements, soon led to the disappearance of the thatched cottages as the houses in the village were rebuilt to more modern and hygienic standards.

This postcard was sent in 1907 and shows, on the right, one of the last thatched cottages in the village. A hundred years earlier most of West Linton would have been made up of such cottages. The washing seen here on the Lower Green would at this time have had to compete with cows, as both village greens were used by the local farmers for grazing, a tradition going back to droving days. On the right, beyond the cottage, can be seen St Mungo's Episcopal Church, built in 1851. Originally, it also served as a school, the alcove on the east being curtained off to form the classroom; the building directly in the centre of the picture is the church's school which succeeded the classroom. In front of St Mungo's, leading from the main road, is Chapel Brae, a steep hill down to the ford across the Lyne Water. On the other side of the main road is another steep hill, Medwyn Road, leading down to it. In the early days of the motor car, children would in snowy weather sledge down Medwyn Road, across the main road – where one of their number would be on the lookout for traffic – and on down Chapel Brae where, with luck, they would be halted by wet snow before they could enter the river.

The land for the bowling green and tennis courts was given to the village by the Forbes family of Medwyn House in the middle of the nineteenth century for a nominal annual feu duty of one shilling. On the right of the picture, beyond the Lower Green, the central range of buildings was a school for 'females and infants' with a schoolteacher's house adjacent. To the left of this the gable end of the Graham Institute can be seen; this is now the village hall, but was originally a working men's institute. On the Lower Green, in front of the schoolteacher's house, stood the village gas works which were run by the West Linton Gas Light Company. It had its origin at a 'Magistrates' Dinner' in 1851 when Mr Lawson of Deepsykehead proposed 'that the village should if possible be lighted with gas'. So, in 1854 the 'gaswork was fitted up and set going', serving at first several houses and later the churches and the street. Never a paying concern, it had a chequered life until in 1902 it was converted to acetylene. After this it seemed to do well and was converted to 'petrol gas' at a later date. It closed when electricity came to the village in 1931.

Even after the introduction of motor vans, horse-drawn vans continued to be used for several years. The surrounding villages and hamlets were dependent on weekly deliveries and Caird's vans would provide this service. One vanman was William Melrose, a man of military habits, who always had his boots highly polished, as this photograph with him on the left shows. For this occasion he seems to have polished his horse's hooves as well! He and his horse must have been a close team, for it is recounted that after finishing his round at Ninemileburn on a Friday afternoon and partaking of a little refreshment, his horse would obligingly trot him home unaided. Besides being a general merchant, Mr Caird also seems to have been the first 'to do the engineering on a car' for behind his shop was a garage and inspection pit. He also sold three makes of 'motor spirit at Edinburgh prices, cycles at manufacturer's prices and hired bicycles by the day, week or month'. On the left is the Bank of Scotland which first opened its doors in the village in 1857 when Mr Alexander was appointed agent.

Always a vital service to a community dependent on horses, the smithy in Raemartin Square was well placed to satisfy this need. This view shows the premises, next to what was to become the Raemartin Hotel on the right, some time before its demolition in 1879. In the background is Trinity Church, which was built in 1784 to replace an earlier church of 1739. It was first called the Meeting House and only later became Trinity Church. It is now a dwelling house with a virtually unaltered exterior.

The hotel building on the right was built in 1789 as a coaching inn to serve the important Edinburgh to Moffat road, which had been 'turnpiked' in 1753. The hotel had adjacent stables which became a smithy probably when the 'new' turnpike road from Carlops to Dolphinton was constructed in 1833. In 1841 the innkeeper was Robert Brown who remained there for at least twenty years. In 1872 it is likely that Alexander Martin, a grocer of West Linton, bought the building for use as a private house and lived there with his sister, Helen Martin. In 1879 the imposing building on the left was built as a hotel, possibly for Gilbert Rae, an aerated water manufacturer of Dunfermline, who, in any event, acquired Alexander Martin's house in 1895 and ran them both as the Raemartin Temperance Hotel until his death in 1924. James Diffey then managed the hotel (although Rae, and subsequently his estate, continued to own it) until his death in 1932. Diffey's three daughters then took over and bought the hotel outright in 1948. The building had the attractive and unusual feature of a roof garden, as can be seen in this photograph from around 1912.

Looking east along Deanfoot Road to open country and the moor road leading to Penicuik, some time before the First World War. William Jackson was one of two bakers in West Linton in 1912, the other being Andrew Drysdale in Main Street. He was also a confectioner making to order 'marriage, christening and birthday cakes' with 'small bread' being a speciality. Surprisingly, he was also an agent for a veterinary product 'Eczemangeme' which claimed to be 'A thoroughly reliable cure for Eczema, Mange and other Eruptions of the Skin in Horses, Cattle and Dogs: sold at 2s. and 4s.' In those days the village streets were lit until the late evening by a few strategically placed gas lamps such as that shown here at the end of Croft Road.

In days gone by the warmth from the fire always made the smithy a popular spot for local worthies to meet and it is said that many village matters were decided here. This smithy in Deanfoot Road replaced the earlier one in Raemartin Square which was demolished when the hotel was built in 1879. The building in this photograph, taken at the turn of the century, remained as a smithy, although incorporated into garage premises, until it was demolished around 1990 to make way for a housing development. The name, 'The Smithy', has been perpetuated as a street name.

Another view of the Gordon Arms, this time taken at the rear from Braeside at the top of Main Street. This lorry may have been local and by the look of the load is destined for Broomlee Station, perhaps with the trunk of a guest who is leaving the Gordon Arms after spending a holiday in the village, whose charms were much appreciated by visitors seeking walks and sporting recreation such as golf, bowls and tennis. The growing motor traffic at this time must have greatly altered the character of the village as passing traffic paused for a stop at the Gordon Arms and the streets became cleaner with the disappearance of horse-drawn vehicles.

The sign on the gable end shows the proprietor of the Gordon Arms Hotel to be Mr Alexander Gordon, who took over the then Hayston Arms in 1895 and renamed it to reflect the new ownership. It is likely that an inn stood here from the middle of the seventeenth century as the road to Moffat was a popular one, especially since the discovery of sulphur springs in that town in 1630, and West Linton would have been the first stop on the way from Edinburgh. However, with the coming of the railway in 1864, West Linton itself became an attractive place for visitors and by 1900 there were six trains each way per day from Edinburgh, at a return fare of only 1/6d. With its commodious extension, the Gordon Arms Hotel was well placed to cater for this influx of customers.

This view of the Gordon Arms Motor Garage in 1928 shows the original stables for the Gordon Arms Hotel little altered. The building at the back, which were once stables owned by a Mr Robb, is obviously a later addition, but the main building fronting onto the street was built around 1833 when the Gordon Arms Hotel served as a coaching inn. Standing in the centre is Mr J.M. Lithgow, owner of the garage, with his son Norman leaning on a Rover Laundalette on the left and Dod Ritchie, a local farmer from Loch Farm, now Mendick, astride the motorcycle combination.

Built as a coaching inn to serve the 'new' turnpike of 1833, the original part of the hotel beside the two parked cars was known as the Hayston Arms Inn. It had stables on the opposite side of the road, which in this photograph, a hundred years after first being used, have become a garage. To the left in front of the telephone box is the exit of the old road into West Linton from Edinburgh now known as 'The Loan.' This was a branch from the 'old' Biggar Road from Edinburgh and ran through the village to Blyth Bridge and Moffat. As the village prospered with the coming of main drainage in 1863 and a piped water supply in 1875, so the inn was extended and became the Gordon Arms in 1895. Bus services first came to the village in 1926 when it was linked to Peebles and Edinburgh by a private company run by Andrew Harper of Peebles. This was taken over by the Caledonian Omnibus Company which itself eventually amalgamated with the Scottish Motor Traction Company (S.M.T.), whose drivers, with their breeches, leather leggings and peaked caps, offered a stylish service to West Linton folk.

During the First World War many country houses in Peeblesshire were taken over as military hospitals and Lynehurst, on the Edinburgh road, was one such place. Built between 1898 and 1901, when piped water was first able to reach this far, this was an imposing building set in two and a half acres of grounds and looking down the Lyne Valley. This photograph, taken outside the front door, shows staff and patients during this period.

Robinsland, formerly known as Bog Farm, sits on land which formed Linton bog, 'a morass of 100 acres' according to the *New Statistical Account*, which was drained by John Hume, who bought the farm in 1805. This marshy area was possibly the reason for the origin of the name Linton which is derived from the Celtic 'llyn', a pool or lake, and the Saxon word 'ton', a village or collection of dwellings. Beyond lies Broomlee Mains in front of which ran the railway from Leadburn to Dolphinton which saw its last passenger train in 1933, the track being finally lifted in 1962. This photograph was probably taken in the 1960s from a spot on the Edinburgh road, where a modern roundabout now sits, and shows the practice of stooking which was soon to die out here with the introduction of combine harvesters. The foreground has changed but the rest is essentially the same pleasant rural landscape that has attracted people to West Linton for many years.

By 1895 the supply of water from the tank on the hillside above Townhead was proving inadequate for the needs of the village and a new scheme to bring water from North Slipperfield was begun. This was completed in 1898 and on 22 August that year Lady Fergusson of Spittalhaugh opened the 'New Gravitation Water Supply'. This gave a green light to developers as water could now be provided to the higher parts of the village. Work on some houses had already started in anticipation of the new water supply and some very grand villas were built along the Edinburgh road at this time. The scene depicted here is the opening ceremony which took place beside the main road bridge over the Lyne Water.

The Community Centre was situated upstream of the main road bridge on land now occupied by the houses of Lyne Park. It was built as the Pantiles Hotel in 1938 and was used as a hostel for the Women's Land Army during the Second World War. It was later bought by Major E.G. Thomson, the owner of Callands estate, and donated by him to the district for use as a community centre. At first it was well used and for many years was the centre for numerous activities both social and educational. However, its popularity waned and after a short spell as the Linton Roderick Hotel it was eventually sold for housing development and demolished. This gathering was for the installation of the Linton Whipman during Whipman Play Week, the annual summer festival which takes place at the beginning of June. This is derived from 'play', as in holiday, which was a privilege given to members of the West Linton Benevolent Society (set up in 1803 and also known as the Young Men's Mutual Society) for men whose livelihood was dependent on managing horses (hence 'whipman').

The golf course at West Linton owes its origin to Robert Millar who, having arrived in the village in June 1863 to take up the post of schoolmaster, had finally managed by 1890 to raise enough support for the formation of a golf club. Having agreed a rental of £5 per annum with Mr Kerr, the tenant of North Slipperfield farm, he set out with a former pupil, T.C. Baillie, to cut the nine holes and mark the teeing areas with logs of wood. (Kerr made this arrangement without the knowledge of the farm's owner, although he later agreed to it.) The inaugural competition took place on Saturday, 16 August 1890, and, as they say, 'the rest is history'. In this picture Alex Dewer, the greenkeeper, is cutting a new hole while the foursome on the ninth green holes out. The hand mower is an old Pennsylvania, a superior model of the time, and was the first piece of equipment bought by the club. The old clubhouse on the right was built in 1892 and the verandah was added later. It stood until recently.

These sheep, pictured on Medwyn Road opposite the junction of the road to Lynedale House, are a reminder of the large sheep markets held close by, possibly in the field to the right, during the times of the great Linton markets of the seventeenth and eighteenth centuries. At the markets' peak upwards of 30,000 sheep would be sold annually and, regarded as the largest in Scotland, their reputation led to the expression of as 'big as a Linton Market' in description of large gatherings. According to Dr Alexander Pennecuik, a local landowner of the 1700s and the author of a history of Tweeddale, at the end of the eighteenth century there was 'a short-bodied, black-faced and legged, horned and coarse-wooled sheep called the Linton breed'. These were sold at the market near Bridgehouse, now Medwyn House, and were then 'driven to the Highlands, Ochil Hills in Fifeshire, etc.' up the drove road seen here and on across the Pentland Hills via the Cauldstane Slap.

Lynedale, the area around Lynedale House (pictured here) half a mile north-east of West Linton, must have seen considerable activity over the years. Since prehistoric times this was a crossing point of the Lyne Water and the Roman road from Clydesdale crossed very near here, as did subsequent roads. The main road from Edinburgh to Biggar also crossed here at one time. Being a day's journey from Edinburgh and at a junction with the drove road over the Pentlands, a dwelling and later an inn had been established here since the thirteenth century when the crossing was known as Biggeresford. Mary, Queen of Scots, passed along this road in 1567 and shortly after this it was recorded that the inn was called Brighouse Inn. The present bridge behind Lynedale House is not as old as this, possibly having its origins in the early eighteenth century when the building seen to the right behind the trees was perhaps a toll-house for the collection of 'pontage' on bridge traffic. The house was owned, at least until the 1890s, by William Sanderson, a Leith wine merchant who used it as a summer home.

Half a mile upstream of Lynedale Bridge on the left bank of the Lyne Water are the ruins of a lint mill which was erected in 1804. The last miller was Alexander Davidson who died in the village in 1858, aged eighty. Lint, or flax, was 'bruised, scutched and heckled' at the mill to separate out the fibre for spinning. Although a short-lived activity, the memory of this mill is kept alive by the singing at local concerts of a setting of Robert Sanderson's poem, 'The Old Lint Mill'.

The messages on many of the postcards sent from West Linton in the early 1900s refer to periods of rain interfering with the holiday pursuits of the visitors. It is not surprising therefore that the hills above the village should be chosen as the site for water supply reservoirs. Baddinsgill Reservoir was made above Baddinsgill House by the construction of a large dam across the Lyne Water. Work started in 1926 and this photograph shows some of the workmen, standing beside a steam crane, who were still employed in the scheme several years later.

One of the oldest and best known inhabitants of Carlops at the end of the last century was William Walkinshaw, pictured here at the age of seventy-eight. Born in Carnwath in 1826, he became a carrier after admiring the relative affluence of a man of that occupation who was lodging at his home. On this 'cadger's' retirement William took over his route from Carnwath to Edinburgh via Carlops, and for cash he would buy the produce of farmers and shepherds and sell it in the market at Edinburgh's High Street. He did not confine his business to these dealings alone and would also accept parcels for delivery at the various points of call on his journey. He also supplied his country patrons with goods which they required from the city. In this work he acquired a reputation for reliability and punctuality and it was said that you could 'time your clock' by the rumble of his cart passing your door. He carried on his trade for over fifty years, working in all weathers without failing once to complete his rounds. He died at the age of ninety-two and was buried in West Linton churchyard.

Before being used as a quarry for roadstone this rock at Carlops, together with the one from which this photograph was taken, were much nearer to the road and apparently only a cart could pass between them. A story arose that two witches, or 'carlines', called Jennie Barry, who lived in a cave near the Old Biggar Road, and Mause, who lived at Kittley Brig, would jump between the two rocks at midnight. Thus, 'Carline's Loup' explains the origin of the name Carlops! Beside the rock is Rock Cottage, formerly Carlops Mains, a small farmhouse built in 1804 and said to have originated as an inn. In later years, it returned to this purpose as the Carline's Head. In the fourteenth century Carlops was on the boundary of lands ceded by Edward Balliol to Edward III of England.

This view of Carlops Church and Ashley Cottages at the turn of the century, taken from the site of the present village hall, is still instantly recognisable. The church at Carlops was formerly the Free Church founded at the Disruption of 1843. In 1900 it became the United Free Church and in 1929 entered the larger union with the Church of Scotland. The lamp outside the church was one of two in the village, the other being at the Well. It was given by Mrs Sowersby, wife of a Leith baker, and later relocated beside the newly built village hall. Maggie Small was the village lamplighter and, armed with her ladder, would light the two lamps each evening. Mr Gear, a retired plumber from London, owned the row of three cottages on the right. He had a striped cat called Peter who would follow him along to Veitch's Hotel and then wait for him to come out.

In 1783 the estates of Carlops and Newhall were bought by Robert Brown, an advocate, who in the following year established a cotton weaving industry and laid out weavers' cottages immediately to the south of Carlops Bridge on each side of the Edinburgh to Biggar road. These cottages, seen beyond the two storey building, which at one time was a hotel, were built of stone rubble with sandstone dressings and some were originally pantiled. They would have had a parlour and kitchen, on either side of a through passage, with provision for box beds. In her booklet, *Carlops Memories* (an account of the village in the inter-war years), Margaret Stone recorded that 'besides the Allan Ramsay Hotel there used to be a temperance hotel [now Valance Cottage] run by Mr and Mrs McGill. Mrs McGill, assisted by her daughters Martha and Isa, gave teas. Four in hand coach parties were a regular sight in the summer; the trippers went down to the Village Green behind Eskside and played games. Mr McGill had a horse and waggonette with which he would bring passengers up from Broomlee Station. It was a slow trot and his charge for the journey was 2/6d.'

A view of the Allan Ramsay Hotel in the motoring age shows it equipped to serve drivers with 'motor spirit', while the transport for the customers, partaking in the 2/6d. tea in the hotel, awaits their return. This view, possibly taken in the 1920s, shows the telephone has arrived in Carlops, although mains electricity did not reach the village until 1938. Carlops Poultry Farm, founded in 1914, did have electricity generated locally from Patie's Mill in the late 1920s and this also supplied part of the village.

The Allan Ramsey Hotel was built in 1792 as a wool store by Mr Alexander Alexander, a weaver from West Linton. He was the grandfather of Mrs Veitch who was proprietress for many years and was a great character by all accounts. She wore a lace cap and was affectionately known as Mother Veitch. The hotel has certainly been an inn since the middle of the nineteenth century when the weaving trade began to fail. Being on the main road from Edinburgh to Dumfries, for many years it provided a change of horses for Croall's stagecoaches and had stabling provision alongside.

A busy scene outside the Allan Ramsay Hotel at the turn of the century when horse-drawn charabancs brought day trippers out from Edinburgh for a visit to the scenes depicted in Allan Ramsay's *The Gentle Shepherd*. These were a short distance down the Esk from the hotel, to which they would return for tea after enjoying the romantic associations of the riverside. Like West Linton, in the years between the wars Carlops attracted many summer visitors who bought or rented cottages in the village. There were a number of families from Leith, some of whom settled in Carlops in their retirement.

In the foreground of this view is Carlops Bridge over the North Esk, the river which formed the boundary between the counties of Midlothian and Peeblesshire. Upstream from the village, on the slopes of Pentlands, the North Esk Reservoir was completed in 1850. This was built for the mill owners on the river to allow them to regulate the flow of water for the satisfactory operation of their mills during periods of low rainfall. Over the bridge on the right is a former toll-house, the first in the county for the Edinburgh to Moffat turnpike road which ran through Carlops. 'The Cottage' beyond provided teas for a while under the name Rosedene Tearooms; in good weather these were served in the garden. In the 1930s the toll-house was occupied on his retirement by Charles T. R. Wilson, F.R.S., originally from Flotterstone, who in 1927 had been awarded the Nobel Prize for physics for his invention of the cloud chamber. On the left is Eskside, built by Captain Tweedie R.N. around 1906 on the site of the cottage occupied by William Walkinshaw, the local carrier, who had lived there for over fifty years from 1849. Beyond the shop and the bicycles is Valance Cottage, a former inn and later a temperance hotel.

Habbie's Howe (Habbert's Hollow), the scene of Allan Ramsay's *The Gentle Shepherd*, was a very popular gathering place for picnics and celebrations during the time of the Carlops Games (which were well attended in the late nineteenth century) and also with visitors arriving from Edinburgh in charabancs. Somewhat altered, this sylvan glade is below Amazondean Farm, about half a mile east of Carlops. The path through the Howe is beautifully overhung with trees and the North Esk flowing alongside provided an additional charm to the walk.

Grange School at Lamancha – built in 1832 through the generosity of Mr James Mackintosh of Lamancha – got its name from the estate on which it was built, Grange of Romanno. This name was changed in 1736 when Alexander Forrester Cochrane, a widely travelled man, acquired the estate. He was a celebrated Admiral of the Fleet and renamed his estate Lamancha as a reminder of his days serving in Spain. For the school's opening ceremony the first pupils assembled at their old school at Cowdenburn and with the teacher, John Scott, and the local landowner, James Mackintosh, they marched to their new school behind Angus Bailie who was playing the bagpipes. The school accommodated seventy-two pupils between 1880 and 1890, and in 1904 an additional classroom, the one at the back with the skylight, was built. In 1957 another wing was added to accommodate a medical room, a cloakroom, and indoor toilets, and an electric heating system was also installed. The decline in the school roll to just nine in 1982 led to its closure shortly afterwards.

This picture is captioned 'Romano Sports, 1913' and it was at this time that the Romanno tweed mill, having ceased to function after providing much needed work for local people, was taken over by Messrs Adams and Linkie as a hatchery for their new poultry farm. The group in the photograph may have been part of an event to celebrate this, but local sports were at that time very popular in most villages. The large 2 cwt. sacks make an unusual scene, but seem to have failed to impress the rather sombre looking gathering.

With the closure of the railway from West Linton to Dolphinton in March 1933 the bridge over the road to Romanno Bridge and the West Water, built by Mr Bouch at the inception of the Leadburn and Dolphinton railway in 1864, was removed. However, the spectacle of vehicles splashing through the West Water remained.

'The largest and best equipped poultry farm in the British Isles' was how Romanno Bridge Poultry Farm described itself in 1917, three years after opening, when it occupied 120 acres of grassland alongside the Lyne Water. Those responsible, Messrs F.E. and J.H. Adams and T.D.M. Linkie are pictured here with family and staff outside the company office in Romanno Bridge. The farm occupied most of the village, with the 'Great Incubator House' being the former tweed mill over the road from the office. By 1922 the farm occupied 300 acres and employed forty staff. During the Depression Adams and Linkie gave up poultry farming, although the farm carried on for a few years on a smaller scale. The mill building has since been converted into houses.

The arrival of Messrs Adams and Linkie in 1913 must have made a considerable impression on the local population. Religious services were held by Adams and his wife and were conducted on their veranda and in their kitchen with such enthusiasm that they attracted a large following. The shop on the left, associated with the Poultry Farm, was at the time of this photograph also selling teas and refreshments. On the right, standing at the junction of the road to Newlands on the left and to Moffat on the right, is a former toll-house built about 1830 when the Edinburgh to Moffat road was improved. Old Romanno Bridge, built over the Lyne Water in 1774, is to the right of this cottage.

This cart and carter, pictured in front of the Romanno Bridge Poultry Farm offices, took milk cans daily from Dovecot Farm to Broomlee Station every morning for the first train, which left about half past seven. There is a tragic story connected with this farm – in 1677 two families of gypsies, the Faws and the Shaws, returning from Haddington Fair, fell out among themselves over the dividing of their spoils. In the ensuing fight several of the Faws were killed and later father Shaw and three of his sons were hanged at the Grassmarket in Edinburgh. To commemorate this incident, Dr Alexander Pennecuik, Laird of Romanno, erected a dovecot in 1683 and had inscribed on a stone of the doorway the inscription: 'The field of gypsy blood which here you see, a shelter for the harmless dove shall be'. It is thought that Dovecot Farm occupies this site.

The arrival in Mountain Cross of the photographer and his carriage obviously attracted attention in what was a peaceful hamlet on the road between Romanno Bridge and Blyth Bridge. In 1793 a seceding congregation was founded here and behind these few roadside cottages was to be found the church and manse of its successor, the United Presbyterian Church. This closed in 1911 and the congregation then added its small strength to West Linton church. The church was subsequently demolished and only the former manse remains, with the cottages, and is now a private residence. This settlement also sits on the old 'Thief's Road' from Hyndfordwell, which was likely a branch of the old road that crossed the Pentlands at Cauldstane Slap which from here ran on south past Callands House, Drochil Castle and Lyne.

An account of Blyth Bridge in *History of Kirkurd* recalls that in the mid-nineteenth century it was known as a Knock-Knowes and consisted of twelve dwelling houses, including an alehouse, mill, smithy, joiner's shop and manse. Some of the houses were occupied by weavers. Indeed, at one time the village was inhabited by such a variety of tradespeople that it was the envy of the neighbouring hamlet Blyth. The mill was built in 1817 and when farmers brought in their corn for grinding no money changed hands. Instead, the miller retained a proportion of the meal for resale to other inhabitants in the area. The unusually high price of grain in the year is recorded on a carved stone panel built into the wall which reads: 'Meal per peck this year 2/6, 1817'. The alehouse extended its trade to become the village shop about 1853 and retained its spirit license for many years. Iron rings still embedded in the wall indicate where customers tethered their horses. The shop was reputed to be able to supply anything from a needle to an anchor and a traveller challenged the shopkeeper one day by demanding a coffin. Unruffled, he led the prospective customer to the back shop and there on the rafters lay a coffin kept in readiness, so it is said, by the forward looking (but pessimistic) shopkeeper.

In 1901, shortly before this photograph was taken, this was the scene of much activity as a water pipe was laid across the valley of the Tarth Water as part of the Talla Scheme to supply Edinburgh with water. Two of the surplus pipes can be seen behind the smart new fence. Upwards of 650 men, mostly Irishmen, were employed in this task and it is also recorded in *History of Kirkurd* that the brisk trade of the little shop and post office erupted with the greatest boom they had ever known – at weekends three hour queues built up as the men clamoured to post and telegraph their wages home to Ireland and to stock up with weekly provisions. Eventually, Monday nights were set aside for the Irishmen's business, which was conducted mainly in the kitchen adjoining the shop. Always regarded as one of the best salmon and trout burns – locals adhered to the claim that Tarth trout are tastier than any other – its banks were seldom without some patient fisherman endlessly plying his rod and stacking the catch in his basket.

The school and schoolhouse at Kirkurd, pictured on the left, were rebuilt in 1773 and for the next hundred years management of the school was undertaken by the church. The Parochial School (Scotland) Act of 1861 caused a meeting of the parish heritors to determine the salary for the schoolmaster. They decided to pay him £45 per annum for which, assisted by his son, a pupil teacher, and his wife, a sewing mistress, he was responsible for teaching forty-three boys and forty-three girls. The track straight ahead leads to Castlecraig estate, originally known as Kirkurd, and it was to Castlecraig on Hansel Monday, a holiday enjoyed by the pupils, that the whole school was dispatched, a class at a time, to receive a batch of buns with a newly minted penny in each one. With the continuous stream of pupils passing back and forth, the excitement reached a point where only extreme self-discipline enabled the buns and pennies to be shown to the teacher waiting at the school. When the procession ended the school was dismissed for the day and the buns were consumed and the pennies borne home as souvenirs of the day.

A postman poses for this photograph taken on a sunny morning outside Dolphinton School at the turn of the century. The school has had at least two major alterations since then. The church underwent a complete rebuild in 1786, but the circular nature of the graveyard suggests that this has been a religious site since very early times. The old village of Dolphinton lay to the south of the present one, between the appropriately named farms of Townhead and Townfoot. In the nineteenth century the development of Dolphinton Estate and the coming of the railway shifted the centre to its present position.

This view of the shop at Dolphinton, taken in the 1930s when it was run by Mr R.W. Steven, was a familiar sight to many motorists, especially later when his joiner's shop in the background became the Beechwood Tearoom and the shop took on the additional function of post office. The joinery business moved to West Linton and continued there until recently. The shop is no longer in business and is now a house.

The building on the left was a toll-house, probably built in 1833 after the new turnpike road from Carlops via West Linton bypassed the original toll-house at Loanend. It was sited to catch any traffic from the old road to Newmill, which branches off to the right. The twelve old Scots Pines at this junction were a local landmark and housed at their base a thriving rabbit warren. Today, the remaining eight trees and the houses opposite – Tollhouse, Twelve Trees and Coneycroft – are a reminder of this bygone age. The road alignment in this photograph is that of the Roman road from Clydesdale, which passed close to the right of the small hill on the horizon, known as Kippit Hill. It was on top of this hill that a stone coffin made of local stone and containing a skeleton was found by workmen who were digging a foundation for a cenotaph for the late Captain Mackenzie of Dolphinton who died in the Great War.